W9-BIH-459

UNICEF
Book of
Children's Prayers

compiled and with photographs
by William I. Kaufman

prepared for English-reading children by
ROSAMOND V. P. KAUFMAN
JOAN GILBERT VAN POZNAK

STACKPOLE BOOKS

UNICEF
Book of
Children's
Prayers

UNICEF BOOK OF CHILDREN'S PRAYERS

Copyright © 1970 by William I. Kaufman

Published by
STACKPOLE BOOKS
Cameron and Kelker Streets, Harrisburg, Pa. 17105, U.S.A.

All rights reserved, including the right to reproduce this book or portions thereof in any form or by any means, electronic or mechanical, including photocopying, recording, or by any information storage and retrieval system, without permission in writing from the publisher. All inquiries should be addressed to The Stackpole Company, Cameron and Kelker Streets, Harrisburg, Pennsylvania 17105.

Library of Congress Catalog Card Number: 74-110477
ISBN 0-8117-1808-5
Printed in U.S.A.

Because the language of a child's heart is universal, the photographs and prayers have been arranged to complement each other according to the meaning of each and not according to the country from which each comes.

Introduction

To understand each person's inner heart is to understand his feeling for his God. When we can accept our individual differences in feeling we are then able to respect the individual's right to worship in his own way. Everyone's God teaches love of life, a feeling for living things, respect for the elements such as sunshine, wind and rain. Yet everyone's God teaches us in a different way.

Most children share certain prayers in common, such as those that speak of love and respect for Father and Mother, Grandfather and Grandmother, Brother and Sister; but in many places children recite special prayers: prayers for the rain to come to countries where there is often a great drought, prayers for stopping the rain in lands where there are frequent floods, prayers for good crops so that the corn or rice will grow and be plentiful and the family will not be hungry, and even personal prayers for winning games or keeping animals and insects from biting.

God gives sweet songs to the birds. He makes beautiful flowers grow and puts the twinkle in the stars. God also gives each boy and girl the power to love.

We need so much love in our world. One way to help fill the Universe with the kind of love it needs is for every boy and girl to say his prayers and to mean them enough to live by them; for all of us to read and come to know and understand the prayers of children in lands other than our own.

And so I give you this book. May your smiles be many, your thoughts be kindly and the love in your heart be enriched as you read these prayers that have been spoken by children from around the world as they reach out in faith for the spiritual comfort which we all seek and which we all need if we are to live together in happiness and peace.

WILLIAM I. KAUFMAN

PR

AYER *of a* FILIPINO CHILD *Living in the* CITY

God, thank you for the nighttime and also the very strong rain this morning. Thank you for our food— rice and bread, meat, fish and vegetables; thank you also for our milk. Bless our food. Bless everybody who is hungry and bless my friends too. Amen.

Philippines

Photo: Ecuador

GOD, CREATOR of

We love our God

And sing his praises every day

Who has made the Sun and the Moon,

And sprinkled twinkling stars in the sky.

We love our God

Who has created this universe with oceans, mountains
  and rivers

Who has made beautiful flowers bloom,

And bountiful trees bear sweet fruit.

We love our God

Who has taught sweet songs to the birds and melodious
  humming to the honeybee.

Who is the giver of wisdom, knowledge and strength,

And the beacon light to show us the right path.

We love our God

Who showers his love and blessings on children and makes
  them intelligent and good.

India

Photo: Rwand

HOLY GUARDIAN ANGEL

Photo: Bra:

Holy guardian angel,
My sweet companion,
Don't abandon me
  by night or day.
Defend my soul,
Guide my life
  so that it will not be lost.

Argentina

O my Lord, may this home be blessed.
May your Bible be revered here
    and your commandments respected.
May all who abide here remain faithful
    to the...Soura...and to prayer.
In all of life only the Lord is to be feared.
May the Lord bless me, bless my parents,
    my teachers and all my fellowmen
    throughout the world.
O my Lord, forgive my wrongdoings
    and bring peace to my soul.
And bring joy and good health
    to my parents who protect me.

Algeria

Photo: Brazil

May
This
Home be
Blessed

The One who speaks with honor and greatness to the people,
The One who has crossed the ocean and come ashore
   with strength and courage,
The Sakya Muni Buddha,*
In that Buddha do I take refuge.

Overcoming craving and desire for acquisition,
Cultivating a taste for the melodious sweetness of life
According to the Incomparable, All-powerful Dhamma,†
In that Dhamma do I take refuge.

To be worthy enough to receive the offerings, welcome, oblations
   and respectful salutations
Of the fourfold duo,‡
The eight persons having attained the path and fruit
   of Emancipation by living according to the Dhamma,
In the Sangha§ do I take refuge.

Ceylon

*Sakya Muni Buddha means Exalted One.
†Doctrine.
‡See the prayer, "Honor to the Exalted One."
§Order of Good Conduct.

I TAKE REFUGE

Prayer

for Protection

God, our Father in Heaven,
Take care of me.
Now that my eyes are closing,
May the angels of God
Who have guided my steps today
Protect me from all peril,
    sorrow and sin.
                    Amen

Denmark
Photo: Sierra Leone

O God, dear Lord, teach us the speech
With which to ask thy blessings!
This day, this night, in dark and light
We thank thee for all thy gifts.

These fruits, these flowers, these trees, these waters—
With all these treasures thou hast endowed us.
The heat of the sun, the light of the moon,
The songs of the birds and the cool breeze,
The green, green grass like a mattress of velvet,
They owe all their existence to thy grace.

Dear God, may we do no bad deed
And to thy teachings always be true.
May we forever breathe the breath of thy love
And every moment be aware of thy presence above.

Pakistan

SPEECH

Photo: Malta

prayer
for
prosperity

Photo: Greece

We beg you, O God,
To rule over this town,
Increase our blessings,
And bring us prosperity.
Amen

Kiswahili, from Kenya

THE RULE FOR LITTLE CHILDREN

All you little children

Must always hear your parents;

All you little children

Need only fear your God.

Elizabeth Muoki*

Kikamba, from Kenya

---

*Mrs. Muoki belongs to the Akamba tribe and does her writing in English, using the traditional folk literature of her people in the Kikamba language as the basis for her work.

Prayer for
unity and

Guard her, O Lord,
  as ever thou hast guarded
This motherland so dear
  whose name we bear!
Keep her in mind,
  whom thou hast made so fair!
May he who rules,
  for wisdom be regarded!
In master mercy,
  in man strength increase!
Protect us all,
  in unity and peace!

Dun Karm

Malta

Photo: Brazil

peace

Modé Ani *

I give thanks unto thee, O living and eternal King who hast restored my soul unto me in mercy; great is thy faithfulness.

Israel

*This is the first Jewish prayer to be said upon waking. There are no specific children's prayers but this devotion is the first one taught to the child as soon as it is able to speak. It is also said or chanted in many elementary schools in Israel in a small ceremony held in the morning before class begins.

O My God, guard my tongue from evil

O my God, guard my tongue from evil and my lips from speaking guile. O lead me not into temptation; keep me far from an evil man and an evil companion; and bestow thy loving kindnesses upon me.

Israel

God, Who removest sleep from mine eyes

Blessed art thou, O Lord our God, King of the Universe, who removest sleep from mine eyes, and slumber from mine eyelids.

Israel

Photo: Costa Ric

O Lord Almighty,
Lord of mountains and trees,
Lord of lightening Spring
And beautiful Autumn,
Lord of pity and mercy,
We worship thee.

LORD OF ALL WE WORSHIP

Lord of mercy,
Lord of multicolor clouds
And the East and the West
And the blue sea and the golden sun,
We worship thee.

O Lord Almighty,
Lord of waters, winds and storms,
We worship thee.

Lebanon

Photo: Turkey

THEE

OFFERINGS TO THE GOD CHILD

Here I bring, Our Lady,
These bald chicks.
I didn't bring them broiled;
I have no coal or sticks.

Here I bring, Our Lady,
Little shells today.
Give them to the Child
When he begins to play.

Here I bring, Our Lady,
This ring of tortoise shell;
So you'll defend the Child
From harm, and keep him well.

Here I bring, Our Lady,
This sheet all finely sewn;
So that you'll protect the Child
From the cold of dawn.

El Salvador

Photo: Greece

Give me, O God, your blessing
Before I give myself to sleep;
And while I slumber,
Watch over all those I love.

For my mother, for my father,
For my brothers, I pray
That you keep them long years
In health, strength and happiness.

Prayer of the

Give solace to the sad,
And health to the sick,
And bread to the needy,
And to the orphan, protection
and a roof.

We all worship you
For all that we owe you;
And as we sleep our last sleep,
We shall awaken in your bosom.

Colomb

Child

Photo: Argentina

Going to Bed

And worship Allah alone. Do not worship anything else with him. And be kind to the parents, to the relatives, to the neighbor who is near and the neighbor who is far, to those who happen to be with us, to those who travel on the way, and to those under your hands. God indeed does not love those who despise others and are proud of themselves.

Verse 36, Chapter 4, Koran

Photo: Pakista

WORSHIP
ALLAH
ALONE

Prayer for winning

One,
    two,
Win the game.
Three,
    four,
In God's name.

Ecuador

Photo: Uganda

a game

I

Leading a thousand men, armed with weapons was Mara, seated on the
trumpeting, ferocious elephant, Girimekhala.
Him, together with his army, did the Lord of Sages subdue by means of
generosity and other virtues
By the grace of which may joyous victory be mine.

II

More violent than Mara was the disobedient, obstinate demon Alavaka,
who battled with the Buddha throughout the entire night.
Him, did the Lord of Sages subdue by his patience and self-control
By the grace of which may joyous victory be mine.

STANZAS

III

Nalagiri, the mighty elephant, drunk and raging like a forest fire, was
as terrible as a thunderbolt.
Him, did the Lord of Sages subdue, sprinkling the waters of loving
kindness on this ferocious beast.
By the grace of which may joyous victory be mine.

IV

The wicked Angulimala ran with uplifted sword for a distance of
three leagues.
Him, did the Lord of Sages subdue by his psychic powers
By the grace of which may joyous victory be mine.

V

Cinca, with her belly bound with faggots, made foul accusations with
harsh words in the midst of the crowd.
Her, did the Lord of Sages subdue by his serene and peaceful manner
By the grace of which may joyous victory be mine.

VI

Haughty Saccaka, who lied, was like a banner in controversy and his
vision was blinded by his own arguments.
Him, did the Lord of Sages subdue by lighting the lamp of wisdom
By the grace of which may joyous victory be mine.

VII

The wise and powerful serpent Nandopananda
Him, did the Lord of Sages subdue by psychic powers through his
    disciple-son Thera Moggallana
By the grace of which may joyous victory be mine.

VIII

The hand of the pure, radiant, majestic Brahma, named Baka, was
    grievously bitten by the snake of tenacious heresies.
Him, did the Lord of Sages cure with the medicine of wisdom
By the grace of which may joyous victory be mine.

# of victory *

Ceylon

Photo: Thailand

* The wise one who daily recites and earnestly remembers and tries to live according to these eight verses of joyous victory of the Buddha will rid himself of
misfortune and attain the bliss of Nirvana.

O Lord,

I thank you for protecting me and my parents during the day. I ask you please to take care of us during the night. And I beg you to make me more intelligent in school, and help me to be more obedient and to follow my parents' words.

In the name of the Lord. Amen.

Elizabeth Muoki

A Schoolgirl's Prayer

Kikamba, from Kenya

Photo: Ethiopia

Little guardian angel,

who knows how to listen to me,

I ask you to tell the One

who takes care of my papa

To protect him forever,

And keep all evil from him.

When he goes to work,

When he returns home,

When he laughs with his children,

When he is troubled. . . .

Little guardian angel,

who knows how to listen to me,

I ask you to tell Him

How much I love papa.

I love him so much that

I don't know how to love him more!

By night or day

Don't fail to protect papa.

Lia Gomez Langenheim

Ask You

Argentina

Photo: Malta

PRAYER
of THE
AlPHAbET *

Glory to the merciful, indestructible, ever present God!

You are all-powerful. Everything on earth revolves about you.

Water creature, land creature, sun, stars, planets and angels

All willingly perform their tasks because you shower

   your goodness upon them.

The destiny of the great and the humble alike is in your hands.

In your eyes, each man is a son worthy of mercy.

Water, land, light, air and sky—all are dependent upon your will.

They have no power and no being but for you.

You bestow riches and happiness. You guide the fate of all men.

You are our strength and our life, the source of all compassion.

You bring high the lowly and cause the mighty to bow down.

You are both the giver and the taker of life.

You are the master of the Universe. We are at your feet.

We are all your children. With our heads bent

   we offer you our devotion.

We have now begun to read. Have mercy on us and grant us success.

Nepal

* In Nepalese each line of this prayer starts with a different letter of the alphabet, and so it is meant especially for small children who are just beginning to learn to read.

Photo: Nep

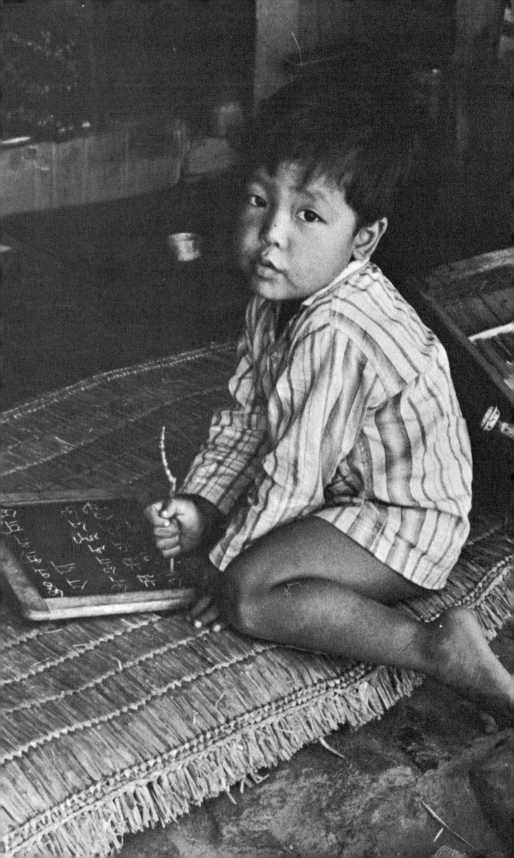

TWO PRAYERS

OF THE

Blessed Saint George,
Safeguard your little animals
So they won't sting
These small children.*

MEXICAN CHILD

Sweet Mother, stay by my side.
Gaze upon me;
Come with me everywhere
So that I am not alone.

Mexico

* Saint George is the patron saint of all little animals, including the insects, both stingers and nonstingers.

Photo:
Costa Rica

PRAYER
of a
FILIPINO
CHILD
LIVING
on a
FARM

Thank you, God, for the rain. It will water our
field and make the rice grow taller today. It will
also make our carabaos happy because they will
have plenty of mud to wallow in. Bless my father
and big brother today as they plow. Bless my
mother and all of us in the house. And please,
do not make the rivers flood because we do not
want the waters to wash away our plants, and
because we want to wash our clothes. Amen.

Philippines

Photo: Philippin

The **A**ngels of

My bed has four little corners,

Four little angels who keep me company,

Two at my feet, two at my head.

The Virgin Mary is my companion,

who says to me, "Lupita, sleep and rest.

Don't be afraid of anything."

Mexico

Photo: Philippin

Lupita

God, our

O God, we have dedicated our hearts
to you,
For we have no other refuge in the world.
In all your goodness, O God, accept
our prayer.
Give us honorable motives.
Provide us with the strength we need to do
our daily tasks.
O God, inspire us to deeds of which we
shall be proud and bless us.
Let us harm no fellowman.
Let us be a source of satisfaction to
our teachers.
Let us be ambitious and willing to work.
Let us be pleasing to our mothers and
obedient to our fathers.
Guide us along the path that will bring
honor to our country and our king,
So that we shall bring delight to
our countrymen,
And so that our earnest endeavors and our
hard work shall bring prosperity to this,
our land.

Iran

Photo: Turkey

refuge

THREE INDONESIAN

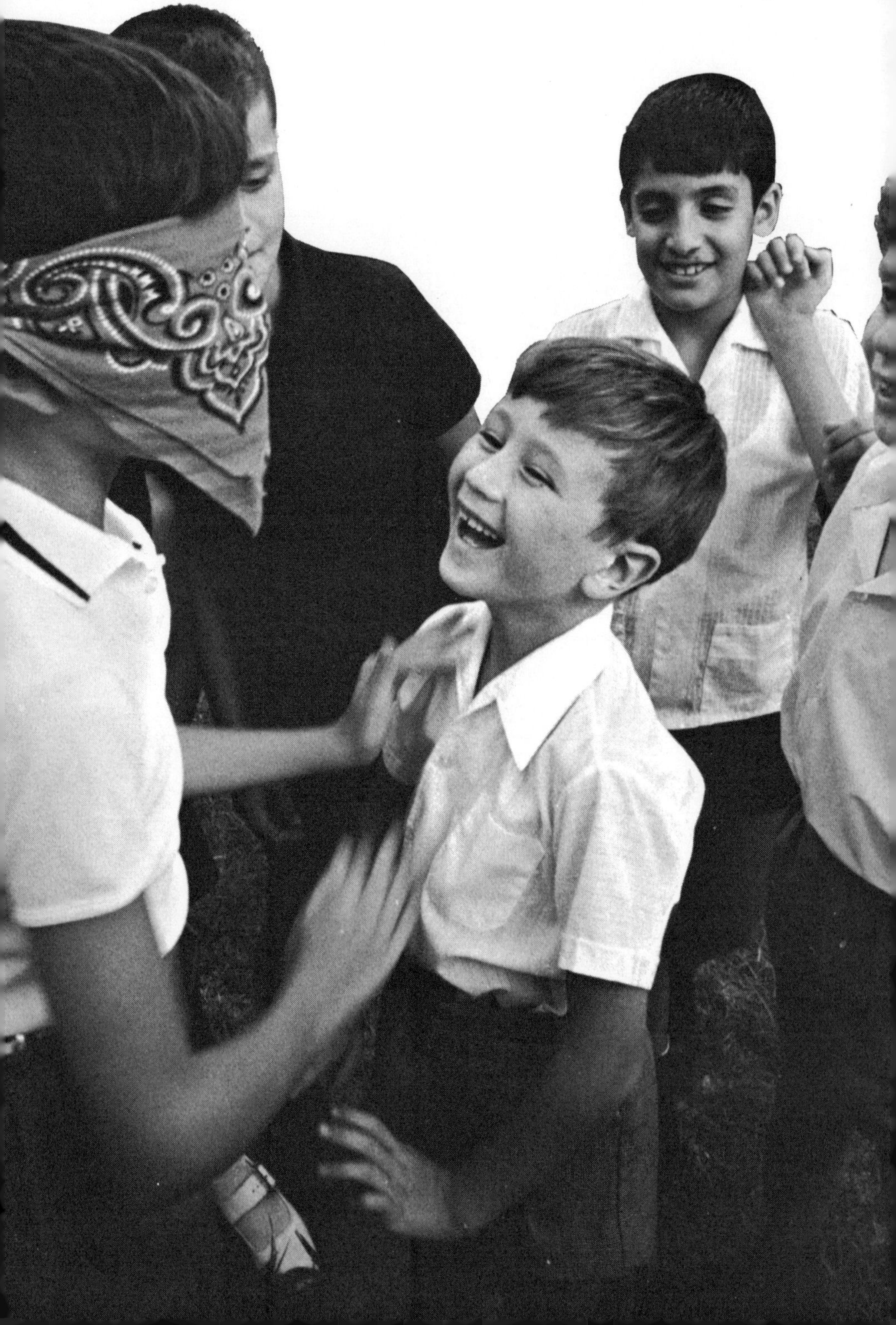

prayers

Upon Going Home

We thank thee, O God, that we are able to
gather with our friends.

Before Meals

We thank thee, O God, for these foods
and drinks.

My God

I thank thee, my God, for all thy blessings.
Protect our parents and our friends.

Indonesia

hoto: Israel

PRAYER FOR
Good Deeds

My God, I offer you
All the thoughts,
Words and deeds of this day.
I ask you to bless me, my God,
And to make me good today.

Mexico

Photo: Venezue

PRAYER AT Bedtime

Now I lay myself to sleep.
To my right side I turn.
Let four angels be witness to my faith and religion.
If I wake up, praise be to the Lord;
If I do not, then may I be consecrated to my faith.

Turkey

Farmer St. Isidore,

Take away the rain

And bring the sun out

Once again.

Ecuador

Prayer to STOP RAIN

Photo: Morocco

Señora Dona Maria

Señora dona Maria,
I come from far away
And I bring a pair of rabbits
To the little Child today.

Squash I bring, potatoes,
And flour for poor Ana.
Mamma, Pappa send regards;
So does old Aunt Juana.

In the crèche of Bethlehem
Are sun, moon, stars galore,
The Virgin and St. Joseph
and Jesus in the straw.

Chile

Photo: Nep

Islamic
Call to Prayer

Adhan

God is the greatest [*repeat four times*].
I bear witness that there is no God but the
   One God [*repeat two times*].
Come fast to prayer [*repeat two times, turning
   face to right*].
Come fast to success [*repeat two times,
   turning face to left*].
Prayer is better than sleep [*repeat two
   times in the morning only*].
God is the greatest of all [*repeat
   two times*].
There is no God but the
One and True God
   [*recite once*].

Koran

Photo: Guatemala

prayer to remove obstacles*

Martyr of Christ,

St. Blaise, St. Blaise,

Let the little bone

lower or raise.

Venezuela

* This prayer is said to children and by children when one of them gets something caught in his throat because they believe that prayer will cause the obstacle to move and save the child from choking.

ANGEL, STAY WITH ME

Holy guardian angel,
My sweet companion,
Stay with me
Day and night.

Costa Rica

Photo: Brazil

WHO is this

I said to my mother,
"Who is this God who is supposed to be everywhere,
Yet is not in our house?
You tell me there is none kinder than he.
You say he is never separated from his creatures.
Why don't I at least see him in my dreams?
Why doesn't he answer my prayers?
I see thee at thy devotions every morning;
Yet I haven't seen him."

My mother answered me gently.
"Seek him in thine own heart.
He is in the color and the fragrance of the flowers.
The spring garden and the blossoms are evidence of
    his Being.
God is in chastity and in goodness.
He can be seen in the rays of the sun.
Trust in God in everything you do, my son,
And do not offend your fellowmen by any act
    of unkindness."

Iran

GOD?

Photo: Kenya

MY
SOLEMN

Photo: Rwanda

PRAYER

O Lord, this solemn prayer comes from deep desire,

May my life be as pure as candle fire.

Let my every breath dispel the world's gloom,

Let my spirit glow so brightly that darkness meets its doom.

May my life enhance my country's glory

As the flower enhances the garden's splendid revelry.

May I be as faithfully drawn to learning

As the moth is drawn to the candle's burning.

May my life be devoted to serving the needy

And to loving a sorrowful, ever suffering humanity.

Lead me away from the path of temptation.

O Lord, let truth alone be my destination.

Pakistan

Homage to God

I have seen the waters flow in the river.

I have seen the flowers along the banks of the river.

Passing by, I have gazed upon the countryside

And inhaled the perfume of the orange blossoms.

I have been grateful to God and I have said thank you to him.

Algeria

Photo: Guatemala

To test Otávio, the teacher
Says, "Come here, you who know all!
Tell me where on the vast expanse of earth
Or in the endless heaven God may be!"

Remaining silent for scarcely a moment,
Otávio soon makes this reply:
"My teacher, I would give
   you anything
If you told me
   where he is not!"

Olavo Bilac

Brazil

God

Photo: Nepal

*HONOR TO THE EXALTED ONE, freed from all bondage, and fully enlightened.

I take the Buddha as my guide.

"He is the Lord, the Exalted One, freed from bondage, fully enlightened, perfect in knowledge and conduct, taking the straight path, who realized the true nature of the world, the Guide and Instructor of mankind, the Greatest Teacher of devatas† and men . . . the Buddha."‡

I take the Doctrine as my guide.

"The Doctrine, well-preached by the Blessed One, brings results, visible, immediate, exemplary, introspective, and to be individually experienced by the virtuous person."‡

I take the Order as my guide.

"The Order of the Buddha is of good conduct, of upright conduct, of wise conduct, of dutiful conduct. This order is of four pairs that form the eight persons called 'Atthapurisa Puggala' (Those who attain the path and fruit of Emancipation) who are worthy of offerings, welcome, oblations and respectful salutation, who are compared to the richest field in which to sow the seeds of merit."‡

Thailand

* This prayer is recited three times consecutively and is used both as a bedtime prayer and a prayer for the Sabbath days. On the second and third recitations, the lines, "I take the Buddha as my guide," "I take the Doctrine as my guide," and "I take the Order as my guide," are changed to "For the second (third) time, I take the Buddha as my guide, etc."
† Demons.
‡ From a book of recitations for the Order of Bhikkhus of Thailand.

Photo: Thailand

Child Jesus,

Docile Little Lamb,
> Make your cradle
> In my heart.

Child Jesus,

You are my love.
> Come down from heaven
> Into my heart.

Little Jesus *of my life,*
You are a child like myself.
That is why I love you so much
And I give you my heart.

Peru

Photo: Costa Rica

Opening Prayer

Fatihah

In the name of God, the compassionate,
    the merciful!
The Lord be praised, Lord of the worlds,
The compassionate, the merciful,
Supreme on the day of judgment.
We worship only you, and to you
    we cry for help.
Show us the straight path
Of those whom you favor,
Of those who do not anger you
And of those who do not go astray.
Amen

Koran

Photo: Singapore

PRAYER

TO STOP A Dog FROM BITING

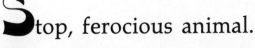

Stop, ferocious animal.

God was born first,

Then you!

Ecuador

H

HOLY ANGEL of the LORD

Holy angel of the Lord,
My never tiring guardian,
If divine mercy
Entrusted me to you,
Always guide and guard me,
Command me and enlighten me.

I pray to you and to all the saints.
Full of joy,
I honor God with a Paternoster
And with an Ave Maria.

noto: Costa Rica

Brazil

Berceuse

Sleep, little child, sleep.

Your brothers are in the fields.

They will bring you ripe oranges

to make you grow strong.

Nighttime is falling.

Sleep, little one, sleep.

The moment for rest has come

and for you I sing,

"Old man, come to close the baby's eyes.

Bring him rest until morning."

And suddenly, in his bed,

The little one

Foufouldé, from Cameroon*

* The prayers recited by most children living in Cameroon today are those of the Christian, the Moslem and the Animist, but in the traditional life of the villages children heard their mothers singing such lullabies as this at bedtime. Reference to the "old man" in this berceuse shows the way in which the patriarchs of the village were thought to have extraordinary influence due to their wisdom and spiritual gifts.

Photo: Hong Ko

sleeps.

PRAYER
of the
CIRCUMCISION

land of the SEREE

Greetings, God!

A moodi!*

May the leader of this initiation into manhood
and I have peace.

A moodi!

May the steward of this initiation into manhood
and I have peace.

A moodi!

May the King of the people of the Sereer
and I have peace.

A moodi!

May the gourd with a handle in which we receive
our nourishment and I have peace.

A moodi!

May the copper pot in which we cook and I have peace

A moodi!

May the he-goat, in contrast to all I have said,
lose his life so that I may have peace.

A moodi!

* So be it.

Senegal

Photo: Ghana

ITE

God is gold.

Let us slumber;

Let us envision

What Mary is doing.

* This is an evening prayer.

GOD
IS
GOLD*

Mary is sitting on a little golden stool,

Holding lovely baby Jesus in her arms.

Little Jesus is watering the lambs,

Guiding little souls toward the holy heavens.

God is gold.

Let us slumber.

Slovene, from Yugoslavia   Photo: Tunisia

Guardian angel,
Sweet friend,

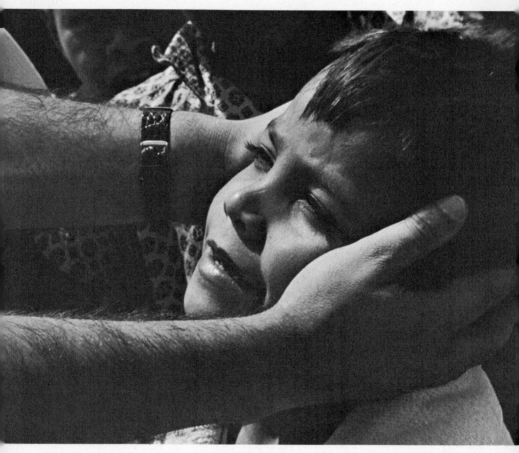

Photo: Costa Rica

Stay with me so I shall not get lost.

ngel

Let me follow in your footsteps.

Angel who leads me,

Stay with me and guard me night and day.

Venezuela

who Leads Me

MORNING

Almighty God, in thy holy name I arise from my sleep to a world bright with sunlight. The vast theater of the world is full of thy glory and every living thing is the work of thy hands; flowers spring forth for thee, fields are ever green, and trees bear fruit. The sun beams down on us and birds praise thee joyfully from the branches of the trees. Even the fish sing thy holy name. On this day we thank thee, Almighty God, Lord of all existence, and pray that you will guide our footsteps so that we may follow thee and live in the precepts of thy law.

PRAYER

Ecuador

Photo: Sierra Leon

Prayer of the German Child

Dear God,

May I revere all that is good and true

So that in heaven

I may draw near to you.

Germany

Heavenly Child Mary

Heavenly Child Mary,

I give you my heart.

With your little hand

Grant me your blessing.

Peru

Photo: San Salvador

Gran

Grant that we lie down in peace,
Secure in thy protecting love,

And shelter us beneath thy wings
To keep us safe throughout the night.

On the morrow raise us up
In perfect peace to life, O God,

To face each task with faith in thee,
Our zeal renewed and strength restored.

Save us for thine own name's sake,
And guard us from all lurking foes.

Remove all sorrow, hatred, strife,
And turn thy children's hearts to thee.

Spread thy tent of peace, O Lord,

that We lie down in Peace

Above Jerusalem, we pray,
And shield thy people Israel,
Dispersed abroad in every land.

Praised be thou, our Lord and King,
Whose sheltering love spreads over us,

Enfolding all who seek thy peace,
Who find their hope and strength in thee. Amen

Israel

Photo: Israel

ACKNOWLEDGMENT

I am indebted to so many for their help and cooperation that it would take a world almanac to include everyone by name who has made this vast project possible. To UNICEF in New York, Paris, and in each of the forty-two countries I visited I am especially grateful. To the ambassadors, ministers of education, ministers of culture and information, consular staffs and members of the staffs of the permanent missions to the United Nations, UNESCO staffs, religious leaders, translators, scholars, individual researchers, writers, parents and staffs of various welfare agencies for children who helped in the collecting of the written material, I say, "Bless you and thanks." I dream that all our efforts will help all our children to a greater understanding of each other.

WILLIAM I. KAUFMAN

about
William I. Kaufman

WILLIAM I. KAUFMAN's love of children and belief that they are the hope of the world have led him to take on the almost impossible task of compiling material and photographing for this volume in forty-two countries. His over eighty books on a variety of subjects are published in English, French, German, Italian,

Swedish, Japanese, Danish, Spanish and Arabic.
Starting in the theater and continuing in television,
he has pursued a successful creative life as a com-
munications executive and consultant, a theatrical
producer, a writer-editor, a teacher, a photographer
and a song writer.

Design by Krone Art Service